The BOM:

Betting On Me

Rob
Welcome to the B.O.M Squad
I hope you enjoy

\#LIFE HAPPENS FOR YOU
\# LIVE YOUR PURPOSE

by
Lynn F. Austin

Lynn Austin
2020

DEDICATION

To my family, the nucleus of the little girl I was and a catalyst for the woman I have become. I love and thank you for our family bond and all the facets of our "us."

ACKNOWLEDGEMENTS

This book would not have been possible without the tireless encouragement and support of my community of account-abilities partners, family and friends.

~ 4 ~

INTRODUCTION

Life is like baking a cookie. A cookie is born when it is separated from a batch of dough by a baker, using her hands, or rolling out the dough and using a cookie cutter. The hands will not be perfect. The cutter may be dented or bent. Therefore no cookie is made perfect, and in fact, one may be badly damaged when it is set on the sheet for baking. But this initial process is not the end. Each cookie endures the heat of the baker's oven and reacts to this heat in its own individual way. And this is what determines the cookie's final shape, and even its flavor.

If your life endures hurt, pain, and disappointment, it doesn't have to stay that way. You can depend on flawed bakers and bent forms, or you can absorb all of the nourishing heat life provides and shape yourself into an aware, attractive, successful person. Not just in terms of material success, but in all of the personal aspects of your life.

This is the story of my beginnings, my trials, my struggles, but mostly my discoveries. It is finally a story of how I overcame obstacles and came to look at myself in a new and different way. It is the story of how I found success in business and in life. Moreover, how you too can see through the challenges in your own path to personal enlightenment and clarity. I wrote it for you, and I sincerely hope it brings you joy.

CONTENTS

CHAPTER 1:

A NEW VISION

I will take my stand at my watchpost and station myself on the tower, and look out to see what he will say to me, and what I will answer concerning my complaint. Habakkuk 2:1

"We have come a long way together, haven't we?" I looked out on my classmates at Columbia Union College, and beyond at their friends and family members that had come to celebrate our achievement. "I never expected to be here. I wouldn't be here if not for a few people who believed in me and encouraged me. I shouldn't be here at all, but I'm not only here, but I am also honored to speak to you.

"It didn't happen all at once. It wasn't easy. We *worked* to get here!" I smiled as applause, and a few cheers rose from my classmates. "But by continuing to take the next step and do that work, the little, everyday work that seems like nothing, eventually we accomplished something significant."

"So remember that you can accomplish your dreams, your goals, and your visions. Persistence and hard work got us this far. Imagine what the future holds if we apply this to all of our endeavors."

"Nothing I can say to you is more important than this: keep striving for the best in the little ways, and by doing so, make your own future. No one else can do it for you, and no one on earth is more qualified for your success than you are. Today, take that persistence on as a full-time job. Excel at it. And never quit that job, as long as you live. Thank you."

The arena erupted in applause. The crowd stood, and I heard shouts of joy and encouragement from my classmates and many others around the room. It was breathtaking. I had expected applause as a courtesy, but apparently, something I said had sparked a flame of enthusiasm. I hoped that I had done some genuine good for those who listened to my speech that day. But what it meant to me was something different entirely. It was the culmination of a lifetime of searching. Of challenges, of misdirection, of losing myself and finding myself again on the other side. By fate or ignorance, or confusion, by a lack of guidance and a presence of invaluable guidance at different times in my life, I had persevered through adversity and found my true place in the world.

That night, I felt that success. Not as a bullet on my resume, or a slogan, or an empty mantra, or even as a number on a bank statement. But as a real validation of who I was. My search had found an end or at least a landing point near the end. I was home. I did not get there accidentally, and home was now a long way from where I began, what was home to me in the beginning.

CHAPTER 2:

HOME IN THE BEGINNING

I woke up to noise, not certain what it was. Then I heard voices. My mother obviously upset about something, and the low voice of my father at the exterior door downstairs. I went to the glass doors leading to where my mother stood at the top of the stairs.

"What are you going to do if you kick me out? What about the kids?" He said.

My mother did not respond, but I knew she was making it clear that my father had done something that she could not excuse. It was late in the evening. She had heard him pull up in his car, and was waiting with a pot of boiling water, threatening him with it. She was trying not to upset us children, but she knew she was doing the right thing and it was the only time it could be done.

"You should have thought about these kids instead of running around making more kids," my mother said in an intense whisper.

Behind the upstairs door, I was confused. I had never heard my mother and father argue before. I could sense something unusually bad was happening. It seemed like it was falling apart.

"You don't know what you're doing, Shirley. But if that's the way you want it." My father's voice was soft and calm as always but laced with an iciness that belied the emotional separation that had been building to this point between him and my mother. I heard the door slam, and his words echoed in my mind and chilled me. Even then, I knew he would not be coming back. Why? Had I done something wrong? Were we so bad he couldn't stand to live with us? Did he not love us?

From that point on, my family was different. For years, my mother supported us with no help from my father. My mother would work several jobs to make ends meet. She would often work midnight shifts at a local factory in Inkster, MI. She would come home in the morning in time to send us off to school. With my mom's hard work along with assistance from her mother and brother, I was able to join the school band and learn to play the flute, at which I excelled. We always had clothing and a roof over our heads, and never went hungry.

A couple of months after my parents separated, my mother got a job at a hospital that paid well enough for her to only work one job. Once she was cooking dinner and sent me on an errand that taught me an important lesson about myself, and shame.

"We're out of milk, Lynn," my mother said. "Come here." She went into her purse and rummaged around, and pulled out two one-dollar food coupons, and held them out to me. "Go down to the corner store and get a half-gallon." She went back to the store, and I walked out into the street of our Detroit area home.

Although we were on food stamps, my mother had been able to purchase a home on Derby Street through a government program, and we had moved there in 1971 when I was about ten years old. Our old neighborhood had been like an extended family. Adult neighbors were extra parents, and the children, extra brothers and sisters, patches on my broken home.

But now I found myself walking down a completely different street to the local store. We were the only black family in this neighborhood, and some of the neighbors did not appreciate what they saw as an intrusion into their hitherto racially pure subdivision. Our house had been barraged with eggs around Halloween. One morning, as we left for school, I saw racial slurs spray-painted on the house by cowardly neighbors under the cover of night. It was the opposite of extended family.

The people seemed as cold as the white paint on the houses, if not downright hostile.

I was ten years old. I did not know whether to be angry or ashamed. As I set the container of milk on the checkout counter, I felt the eyes of the cashier on me.

"Eighty-nine cents," she said, glancing at the line formed behind me. I was already different. I was already standing out in an all-white neighborhood. I had a few dollars I had made doing odd jobs for family and neighbors. I did not want to give her the food stamps, so I shoved them deep in my pocket and handed a dollar of my own money to the cashier.

"Eleven cents is your change," she said coldly, handing me the coins and turning to smile at the white lady behind me.

So much in my life was beyond my control. So many hurtful things. But even I could change something, and I knew it, and I had done it. I had a few dollars of my own money, used it, and did not have to face the shame of using food stamps.

I never told my mother that I had not used the food stamps that day. My mother was doing the best she could, and I did not want her to know I was ashamed of having to use food stamps. But I learned that I felt ashamed of not having my own money and having to rely on public assistance. I wanted money of my own, so I could stand tall, feel proud and have nothing to be ashamed of.

I was a child. I did not know much about money at all, and I did not know what I could expect in life. I could not conceive of great wealth, or being the owner of a business. I only knew that I did not want to be on food stamps, or have people look at me as if I was something less, something not as good as they were, as if I were outside the window with my nose pressed to the glass. With the exception of my grandmother and uncle, very few people were showing me that I could be anything. That there were endless possibilities for achievement that were mine for the taking. Some others seemed to be telling me just the opposite: that I was not good enough, and never would be.

Lynn F. Austin

CHAPTER 3:

POISON

Things were not all bad growing up, even in the new neighborhood. We had a nice house of our own. We went to softball games on Saturday mornings with the local church, and in the summer I went to Vacation Bible School. My father did not come around, nor did we visit him. I saw my grandmother and my uncle often. They were the only ones that really encouraged me growing up. My grandmother would say you can be anything you want, but you have to be prepared for the opportunity when it comes. I remember once she signed us up for boater safety lessons so that we would know our way around a boat--a boat we didn't have. Although sometime later -- in my late twenties most of my friends had boats -- 26ft or bigger. I was often among "the crew," partly because I had a boaters license and "knew my way around a boat." My uncle was a school teacher and would travel the world, bringing back stories that create a desire in me to travel and see the world. He always stayed on me about my studies. Occasionally he even taught the same grade I was in. He would push me to excel. I loved it.

My mother never really had men she was dating around us growing up - or even come to the house for that matter. But one day, the front door opened, and I heard my mother laughing. There was a man with her. His name was Tharmond. While they never married, we came to refer to him as our stepfather.

* * * *

"Listen," my mother whispered, as the three of us sat with her at the breakfast table. She spoke in a low voice to avoid her boyfriend hearing the conversation. "Tharmond did not finish high school. He wanted to, but he had to quit school to help his mother provide for the family." He works hard, and he is a good provider. Then she looked at each of us, looked sternly into our eyes.

"Don't *ever* mention this. He's very sensitive about it, and there's no reason for any of us to bring it up. Understood? This is very important because he will get mad at me for telling you." We finished our breakfast, fully understanding that we were not to mention this and doing so would upset Tharmond, and that would be unpleasant.

* * * *

It was very rare for us to see my father, but after the divorce was finalized (six years in the making) there came a day when we did. One day he picked us up to spend the day with him. He was taking us to the beach. All day leading up to my dad coming to pick us up, my mom and Tharmond argued. I didn't really know for sure what they were arguing about, but it had something to do with my dad coming by to pick us up.

"Let's go kids!" my father said, standing by the car. My brother Darryl, my sister Iranette and I piled into the car and we pulled off for a day at the beach, with my dad. At the beach, we met a woman and her two kids – a little boy and girl. We had no idea they were our siblings. We just thought they were this woman's kids. I remember after getting out of the lake, she taught me about using conditioner after I washed my hair. My mom did not appreciate me mentioning that Ms. Loretta said I should use conditioner in my hair after I wash it so that it would be healthy. I didn't realize at the time that Ms. Loretta was the woman my mom and dad had argued about back when I was five, standing in the doorway. Ms. Loretta had also gone to High school with my mom and dad. And she had two children, Jon and Enre.

That day at the beach was a day of fun. I didn't care who the children were. I enjoyed being with them, being with my dad and having a good time. And I didn't know that while we were out having fun, the opposite was happening back home. What started as an argument had escalated into a huge fight. We returned home to the next in a series of long, ranting arguments, with my "stepfather" doing most of the ranting.

"How can you let that man take your kids? He didn't even claim Iranette as his own in court!" Tharmond shouted. "What kind of mother are you to do that?" "I'm more of a father and provider for them than he has ever been!" He shoved my mother into the wall, and she fell to the floor.

Eventually, he packed his things and stormed out of the house with ALL of his things in bags, boxes and whatever he could put them in. But, sure enough, he would return, and it would not be the last time he would leave, return, argue and physically harm my mom – then repeat the cycle all over again.

CHAPTER4:

IMAGES

I could hear a lot of noise and carrying-on in the living room. My mother, my uncle and some friends were having a good time talking, catching up and enjoying each other's company. I was in the back room with my brother and sister. We lived in Motown, and sounds of Marvin Gaye, Smokey Robinson, and the Temptations drifted throughout the house. I heard laughter. I went into the kitchen to get something to drink. In the kitchen, there was a strange odor, it smelled like gas, but I wasn't sure. There was a gas leak somewhere, so I went to tell my mom.

"Ma! I smell gas!" I said, timidly walking into the living room. I knew that I wasn't allowed to be around "grown-folks'" conversations. My mom would not be pleased with me inter-rupting!

"What are you doing in here? You know you're not sup-posed to be in the room when adults are talking." My mother turned back to her guests. I left and went back into the kitchen to be sure. It was definitely gas! I looked down and walked back into the living room. I knew I was right. My mom went into the kitchen, opened the oven door, then went back into the living room saying that she didn't smell gas. I guessed it was not important enough for me to say anything else and I did not want my mother to yell at me again, or to embarrass her in front of everyone, so I turned around and left.

I walk into the kitchen, where food was cooking in the oven. I clearly smelled gas, and opened the oven door to prove it! Instantly I felt a stream of heat on my face and smelled hair burning. My face was burning, and my hair was on fire.

"Oh my God!" my mother shouted as she and my uncle ran into the kitchen. Somebody turned off the oven, while my mom was beside me and my uncle put the fire out in my hair. But it was still stinging, and I could feel the heat on my face and smell the unmistakable scent of burning hair and human flesh.

"Am I going to die?" I said, my whole face stinging from the pain as my uncle finally got the flames out. I could not see through my damaged eyelids. They rushed me out, terrified, not knowing what to expect, to the car. There Tharmond was sitting with the engine running. While my mom consoled me, he drove faster than I have ever seen him drive.

"It burns!" I cried, horrified. I had never had anything this bad happen to me. I was in shock. My hands were cold. My face still pulsed with pain, and I was afraid to touch it.

"Everything's going to be alright. They'll take care of you. Don't worry. You're going to be fine." My mother struggled to sound calm, but she was clearly as scared as I was.

* * * *

"Don't worry. She is going to be okay," the doctor put his hand on my mother's shoulder. A look in his eyes suggested that he knew her and that we had been treated differently because of that fact. I was not very aware of what was going on. I was also in shock and unable to think clearly, and they had given me some strong pain medication. "What about her face?" my mother asked.

"The damage is significant, and she'll probably need plastic surgery. We won't be able to determine to what extent for about six months," the doctor said. "I'll have several prescriptions for you, ointment and antibiotics. The rest is just time that she needs to heal."

"Thank you, doctor," my mother said.

"You're welcome," the doctor said, turning his head as he pulled the door open. "She's very fortunate that you knew what to do and acted fast. You should be proud of that." My entire head was covered with bandages. I felt like a mummy. I don't remember much of anything else that day, but we went through the checkout paperwork, and I had a wheelchair ride to the car. When I got home, I was very tired and went to bed.

* * * *

After a few days, I was feeling more alert. We were able to remove some of the bandages, and I could see a little. I got up out of bed and went into the bathroom. My mother had covered the mirror by taping newspaper in front of it so that I could not see myself. I moved part of the newspaper, and carefully, out of the side of my eye, glanced at my face, still half-scared to look.

I was horrified. I had never seen burns like that. My face was covered in mutilated skin and scabs. I felt so bad that I cried, and the tears stung the raw wounds on my face. I looked like a monster.

* * * *

We always had dogs when I was growing up, and I loved them. My favorite was Black Panther, Panther as we called him. He was a beautiful, jet-black Labrador retriever. He roamed freely in the house, and I would often play with him, tease him and pet him. He was the best.

One day I saw Panther asleep on the floor in the dining room of our house. His legs were twitching like he was having a bad dream. I sat on the floor next to him. I was petting him, and trying to tease and wake him a little too. I must have teased him a little too much. He came out of his sleep all of a sudden and snapped at me. I had no time to move and he sunk his teeth into my chin and upper lip.

My mother took me in for another visit to the emergency room at Henry Ford Hospital and stayed with me as the doctor put 43 stitches on my face. Panther had torn a muscle in my lip. My lip hangs slightly on the right side to this day.

I healed from all my injuries, with only minor permanent damage, but it took many months. Tharmond wanted to have Panther put to sleep for biting me, but I cried and fought to keep my dog. I knew he didn't mean to hurt me. From that day he was extremely protective of me. I was tucked away at home doing my assignments remotely. At the time, I did not understand what a great accomplishment it was to do my school work with so little help. My uncle, the school teacher who often taught my grade level, would also give me extra work assignments to help me stay ahead of my class.

* * * *

When I was twelve years old, Mom was injured seriously in a car accident. She had surgery on her leg and needed several months to heal. She had a metal rod put into her leg and had difficulty relearning to walk and get around. During this time, she also started to gain some weight. Tharmond would often call her derogatory names, demean her, and cheat on her; this would often result in their arguments where time and time again, he would leave, come back, "confess" to having another woman and return.

"Where were you last night?" my mom would ask.

"Where do you think?" Tharmond said smugly. Tears filled my mother's eyes.

"Can't you see what this does to me? Why do you keep humiliating me?"

"Look, you're old, fat, and ugly. I can have better, and I do. If you can't handle that, I'll just go." Tharmond began to pack his belongings yet again. I saw my mom becoming very different from how she had been before Tharmond. My mother just sat and cried.

The next morning, Mom would either be in a bad mood or be vowing never to let him come back. Then he would come back. The more he left, cheated or they argued, the more my mom began to demean and body-shame me. Mostly in the way

I walked, how I dressed or what I wore. If I was wearing a pair of jeans that I really liked, a style that was very popular at the time, she would start it on me.

"What's that you're wearing?" My mom would ask.

"My new jeans," I smiled, posing. "Do you like them?"

"Like them? You look like a whore!" The smile left my face.

I can't wear them?" I asked. My mom would look away.

"You look like a slut out walking the street." I later found out that Tharmond, who was much younger than my mother – 7 years, would say to her that I looked better to him than she did after she had gained weight and that he could have me. This affected her so much that by the time I was in high school, she only allowed me to wear what she picked for me and a pair of men's jeans that I altered to fit. I don't know that it bothered me that I could not wear jeans, but it did bother me the way my mother treated me and how I began to feel about me and my body.

When it was time, my mother took me to a gynecologist for my first check-up. Her name was Dr. Rebecca Williams. She was very kind and said I was in perfect health. But after the exam, as the doctor was leaving, my mom walked into the hallway, and I heard her speaking to Dr. Williams.

"I want you to write a prescription for birth control pills for her," she said like she was giving the doctor an order. The doctor smiled.

"Mrs. Bonner, there is really no need for that. She isn't sexually active, and has no problems with her menstrual cycle."

"I don't care!" my mother said, getting more agitated.

"There are side effects, you know—"the doctor started, looking a bit concerned.

"I want her on birth control pills. I'm not going to tolerate a teen pregnancy!" My mother eventually got her way, and the doctor wrote the prescription. I felt like my mother was treating me like a slut. She had called me that before. It had nothing to do with my actions. I didn't understand it then, but my mother was reacting to her relationship with Tharmond. But in my adolescent mind, I felt my mother was ashamed of me and didn't want me around. She was the one I looked to. She was the one I was betting on to help me understand my place in life.

The derision of others and the circumstances surrounding me left me doubting my self-worth. My early years were wrought with challenges that would continue to affect me in my early adulthood. I did not know at that time that my best bet was me and my ability to take in everything I experience to move me forward to the next phase. I had so much going for me: talent, intelligence, generosity, beauty! But I could not see these things. I saw the reflection of myself in how others around me – namely my mother - treated me. I was betting on family to define my self-worth, self-image and life purpose. I didn't realize it then, but those things lie within – not outside of me. I only needed to take my life experience, circumstances, and opportunities and stand on them to get to the next level. Betting on my family provided a place to live, food to eat, support through grade school and an appreciation for achievement.

Lynn F. Austin

CHAPTER 5:

DARKNESS

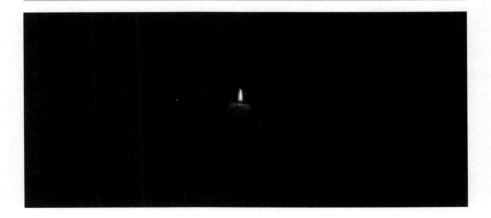

As adulthood approaches, things always get more serious for teenagers. Societies have always had ceremonies and rituals to mark the move from childhood to adulthood. Jewish teens have Bar Mitzvahs and Bat Mitzvahs. Latinas have Quinceaneras. In North America, the Sweet Sixteen party sometimes marks this special birthday in a girl's life. As my sixteenth birthday approached in September of 1977, my mother and Tharmond had agreed to let me have a party at our house. I sent out invitations to all my friends at school and got many RSVPs'.

It was going to be great. But the dysfunction in my family began to get in the way of my plan Sweet Sixteen party.

Once again, my mom and Tharmond began to fight. I don't think it had anything to do with the party, or me, or my brother and sister. But for some reason, after this big argument, I was told that the party was cancelled. I was devastated. I was very shy, introverted and insecure at that time, and the embarrassment was almost too much for me to bear. I was feeling the weight of this, and of everything that led up to it: the way my mother would comment about my body, the violence and abuse Tharmond subjected my mother to. It was all just too much, and the cancellation of my sweet sixteen party was the final blow.

I could not see a way forward, so I thought I had found a way out. I wanted to go to sleep and not wake up. Not deal with any of it anymore. I decided to end my life. I found my mother's pain pills and took them to my room. I wrote a note with tears in my eyes. I took a handful of the pills and lay down on my bed to wait for the end.

Fortunately for me, I did not succeed. My mom found my note. She came to me, waking me and identifying the pills and quantity I had taken. She made me get up, walk, drink fluids and stay awake. I'm not sure why, but she did not take me to the Emergency Room. I guess I had taken enough pills to knock me out, but apparently not enough to do any real damage.

I talked to my mother. She later had a conversation with my father. Together, we decided that I would go live with him for a while. But before that, my mom and Tharmond allowed me to have my sweet sixteen party after all. It was strange, re-inviting everyone after I had canceled, but it turned out to be a nice event, most of the people I had invited eventually showed up to help me celebrate my sixteenth birthday, we danced, ate and listened to great music -- and they all had a good time.

* * * *

I lived with my father for about a year – until his new wife, Alayne, decided it was not such a good idea. It was good for a while, but then it was as if she was jealous or insecure about me being there. She also suspected my dad of cheating and me of keeping his secrets. I moved back to my mom's house.

There was a time, while living back at my mom's house, when my brother and I went out to a party at nightclub and met up with friends. We decided to ride together so we took my car. A car I had saved money to buy. While at the nightclub, I met up with a number of friends from high school. My brother connected with a young lady who needed a ride home. We decided he would take my care and I made plans to get a ride home with some of my former classmates – one in particular had a car. He dropped each of my friends off along the way. I lived the farthest and closest to his house so he planned to drop me off last. Along the way, he said he had to stop by "the office" to pick up some papers he needed for the next day. We stopped by this office building located off of the service drive of the John C Lodge Freeway. He suggested I come in but that he would only be a moment. We entered the building. Once inside, he set the alarm and invited me to have a seat on the couch in the waiting room. Shortly thereafter he said, "I'll just be a few minutes" and called me into the office he was in. Once in the office, he forced me down onto another couch in the office. I pleaded for him to stop, but he raped me. For years, I never spoke about the rape to anyone except my girlfriend Chiquita. She was one of my best friends and the only one I felt would understand and relate to what I had experienced. Back then, living in my mom's house, I felt ashamed. I could not tell her. I kept these things to myself. I did not want them out in the open. I felt as if it would only confirm all the names she called me. The logic makes no real sense and is difficult to explain to anyone who has not experienced rape.

The physical injuries were minor, but the psychological damage was overwhelming. I felt shame and anger and disappointment and things I cannot even describe. This event and the emotions around it impacted me severely through the years and became a part of my thinking about myself. I thought I was "less than." I thought I was never good enough. I felt like I must do things to deserve to be hurt. I thought I was not worthy of love.

The dark events that befell me as I approached adulthood affected me for the next twenty years. I accept my childhood for what it was. It was not all good, and it certainly was not all bad. As a child, betting on your family to help you understand you ... just seems like what you're supposed to do. And in many ways, I guess it worked. I was cared for physically – I had a home, food, and clothing. I got an education. I learned the need and desire for financial independence. This would all carry me forward to my business career and a greater education on how to invest in myself.

CHAPTER 6:

INVISIBLE HEROES

I waited patiently for the LORD; he turned to me and heard my cry. Psalm 40:1

As I neared graduation from high school, I had excellent grades. I took advanced classes, was inducted into the McDonald's All American Marching Band, I wanted to be a lawyer of all things. So I, of course, I was interested in college. I had a school counselor – Mrs. Jones – who sat in her office and asked why

I wanted to go to college since all I could reasonably ever hope to become was to be a housekeeper, a secretary or housewife. To her, college, for me would only be a waste of time, money and effort. It's strange to think that her words could have impacted me that much, but they did. This information stayed with me for many years. I applied to several colleges, but I knew my mother didn't have money for college. I didn't have money for college either, and I didn't know about available programs to get money for college—these were things I should have gotten from my counselor, but I didn't so. I did not put too much effort into going to college. Somewhere inside, maybe I was afraid of failing or afraid the counselor had been right. Betting on others, allowed me to blind myself to the truth about me. I replayed the lies others had told me about myself until I did not only believed them, but told them to myself continually. I had been an A student in school, in advanced classes. I was the first-chair flutist and section leader in the concert and marching bands throughout middle school and high school. There was no reason I couldn't succeed in college. And if I could do that, I could certainly succeed elsewhere. But I didn't know that yet. I needed to be taught and shown.

The people who showed me the potential in myself – who made me see that I am a good bet—I call *Invisible Heroes*. I call them that because everyone who succeeds needs encouragement. It is a necessary ingredient for excellence because, without motivation and encouragement, an individual is less likely to do the hard work necessary to achieve great things. We often see the finished product: the CEO, the Best-Selling Author, and the Olympic Gold Medalist. We know the individual has worked hard to get to that point. But their fame often outshines the people who helped get them there. The necessary ingredients so to speak, are invisible like butter is invisible in a delicious cookie.

The first heroes were my mom when I was younger, but then my grandmother and my uncle. They were the ones during my childhood that told me I could be something more. They encouraged me by telling me that I could be or do anything I wanted if I prepared and put my mind to it. Another was my band teacher in high school, Mr. Latimer. He once called me the "Grand Diva" after winning a section leader challenge prior to a concert performance. I did not really know what a "diva" was at the time, but I took it to mean *especially talented* since I was never beaten in a challenge and remained section leader throughout high school.

I started working at an early age helping my brother with his paper route and still did quite well in school. I even took college preparatory coursework but after graduating High School, my mom helped me to get a job in a coffee shop at Henry Ford Hospital, and I continued to live at my mom's house. I made $360 a month. My mom charged me $180 a month in rent starting with my first paycheck. By that time, my mom and Tharmond had a set of fraternal twins--my brother, Tharmond, Jr. and Sister Stefanie. There was still a lot of chaos in the house, and I resented her for taking that much money from me and having to live with the daily confusion in that household. So I got an apartment and a roommate. My rent was only $150 a month including utilities, and I got to live without the day-to-day drama of Tharmond, my mom and living in that house. I was happy to be supporting myself so that I could live on my own.

Then in 1989, I went to work as an executive assistant for a vice president at Henry Ford Health System, Vinod Sahney. Himself a PhD, visiting faculty at Harvard University, Case Western Reserve University, and professor at Wayne State University, Dr. Sahney was insistent that I go to college. He told me I was smart and intelligent, that I had the attitude and ability to succeed and that I should apply myself in college so that I could use my talents to get promoted to more responsible roles. He told me I was simply too smart not to have a college degree. He nagged me daily. He was so insistent about the matter that I enrolled in evening courses at Wayne State University--one class per semester--just to get him off my back. Reflecting back, I could not be more grateful for his nagging, insistence and care. He saw something in me that others had not or did not know how to ignite: the potential to do something more. Not to *be* something more, but to see a glimpse of my true self, which was something more than I believed I could be. I began to believe that at least a part of me was worth something.

Thanks to Dr. Sahney's prodding, support and encouragement, and confidence building, he gave me additional responsibility in his office; I looked for a step up. While working at Henry Ford Health System, Dr. Sahney had responsibilities for all strategic planning and marketing. I later moved on to the philanthropy office where I was responsible for a program that raised funds for cancer education and research. Much of the fundraising I was responsible for was through the Van Patrick Memorial Foundation, where I was very successful, raising a million of dollars toward a $10million capital campaign for cancer and an endowed chair in the cancer research division of Henry Ford Hospital. While there, I also got a special appointment from the President of Henry Ford Health System— Gale Warden – to work for three months with the White House on the 1994 Government of 7 (G-7) Jobs Summit in Detroit. Working with the White House was an amazing experience, and I learned a lot about White House protocol, social secretary processes, public relations, advance teams and secret service sweeps. These experiences helped me move into a new position in a completely different company, with the Government Affairs, Public Policy Division at Ford Motor Company, and shortly after that, I was promoted to Special Executive Assistant to the Vice President of Washington Affairs with responsibilities for managing Ford Motor Company's presence in Washington, D.C. The move to Washington, D.C. was a big step. This was a whole new world for me. I had lived my whole life in the Detroit area. The weather in the Washington, D.C area was much more to my liking, but more importantly, the culture was amazing, alive and even vibrant. I worked and lived around people who believed in themselves and wanted more from life. They did not always go about getting it the right way, but their ambition was quite contagious. And I caught it!

Lynn F. Austin

CHAPTER 7:

A FORMULA FOR SUCCESS

I was now working for a fortune 100 company, and I was a rapidly advancing into a businesswoman of sorts. I was in a new city with a different culture. But the most significant change for me was that I was in charge of my environment and enjoyed drama-free living. My grandmother had told me I could go anywhere and be anything--I only had to be prepared when the opportunity presented itself. Dr. Sahney's influence and guidance in getting prepared would always be with me. He showed me that I was smart, talented and could succeed on my own. He backed up his words of encouragement with trust and confidence in me to manage my own projects and people. But like any good mentor, he set me free. Like a young chick being pushed out of the nest, I had to fly or fall on my own.

I was prepared and armed with knowledge and know-how, but it soon became apparent that one thing I still had to learn was office politics. Working at Henry Ford Health System and in the nonprofit sector, I had seen office politics, but I think I may have been buffered from the worst of it by Dr. Sahney. At Ford Motor Company, and especially in a place like DC, politics were everywhere, not just in the halls of Congress. I learned my lessons the hard way, surprised when co-workers tried to dominate me, conspire behind my back, and take credit for work that I had done. I was stumped initially, but fortunately, I learned to navigate the system and along the way. I also found out I was made of strong stuff. I would not give in and was determined to make my way in the business world. As one of my favorite authors, Jack Canfield said in his bestselling book *Chicken Soup for the Soul*, "It's not what happens to you, it's what you do about it."

Now living in Washington, D.C., I had seen that I could be successful, that I was smart and capable, and that I could improve myself without failing as that high school counselor had predicted years ago. Determined and taking Dr. Sahney's advice to heart, I worked full time during the day, and also took a full-time course load at Columbia Union College at night. And as the twenty-first century dawned, full of promise, in 2000 I completed my Bachelor of Science in Business Administration, graduating Magna Cum Laude, Vice President of my class, and gave the commencement address at my graduation.

Armed with a new degree and valuable, if sometimes painful, experience, I set out with what I thought was a formula for business success. But I was still learning lessons the hard way about how I fit in the workplace, about the value I added. I wanted to be viewed and respected as a professional. Intellectually, I knew I was not to blame and not at fault in the rape. But my emotions told a different story. Like a torn cookie from a dented cookie-cutter, I clearly had not finished the baking process. My mother's misguided efforts to make me ashamed of my sexuality contributed too. Sexuality is a facet of every human being. But to me, my sexuality and my femininity were the weaker parts of me ...and just things I had to cover up and overcome to succeed. Most often, I tried to pretend this aspect of me did not exist. But the truth kept hitting me in the face. I tried to separate my femininity and professional life, but I think people always perceived there was something beyond the layers that I wasn't revealing about who I was. In a way, they were right. As I look back with a realistic and objective viewpoint, I can see that everyone else saw a smart business *"woman,"* not just a smart business *"person."*

Still, at this point, I was a very effective project manager. I continued to improve myself and found new mentors within the company to help me progress along my career track. From D.C., I moved to Mahwah, NJ, and later I moved to Irvine, CA and was promoted every two years from New Dealer Launch Program Manager, to Cultural Marketing Manager to Brand Manager for Aston Martin Jaguar and Land Rover.

At one point, while working as Cultural Marketing Manager, I was appointed by the company President to a special Executive Level Diversity Advisory Board. This board consisted of the President and Executive Vice Presidents at Aston Martin Jaguar, as well as nationally known leaders of business and industry like the late Julian Bond of the NAACP, Butch Graves of Black Enterprise Magazine, Christy Haubegger of Latina Magazine, and Anna Cabral, who later became United States Treasurer with her name on US currency. It was a big deal, and I achieved great success in my work on the board. I had found a way to focus intensely on the task in front of me, to great effect, but I did not have a real plan for what I wanted in life beyond work.

I learned to live by what I will call a "success by accident" formula based on successes I had achieved in my past projects. It involved a six-step plan that was basically:

1. Set the Objective.

2. Define the Strategy and tactics

3. Execute the Plan.

4. Understand the Impact.

5. Measure Results.

6. Repeat or Replace.

I used this formula and reused it, and it worked well for me. I was promoted to progressively more responsible positions. My final assignment at Ford was as Brand Manager for Aston Martin, Jaguar and Land Rover. In 2006, Harley-Davidson offered me an opportunity to move from Irvine, CA to Milwaukee, WI. An opportunity to go from four-door luxury cars to two-wheel exclusive motorcycles. I said no--three times! But they kept coming back. I prayed about it saying "If this is what I'm supposed to do, everything will fall into place." I guess the third time's the charm. When Harley returned to recruit me a third time, I countered the offer as presented and they matched it. I took my brand and my marketing success to Harley David-son in May of 2006 as Director of Consumer Marketing with responsibilities for outreach markets. I was the first African American to hold such a position in the company.

I had returned to the Midwest, this time headquartered in Milwaukee. Financially and professionally, I had achieved more than I ever thought possible – certainly more that Mrs. Jones thought I would. But I had ignored an entire side of myself. I moved into a newly renovated area in Milwaukee called The Third Ward. I bought an amazing condominium on the river. The view from my living room looked as if I were sitting on a cruise ship. While living in California, I had become quite the real estate investor. I owned investment properties throughout the US and had amassed a net worth greater than $1.2 million. And this would lead me to my next place of growth, develop-ment, and insight.

Lynn F. Austin

CHAPTER 8:

SHADOWS

By the time I moved to Wisconsin in 2006, I had reached a level of success in my career I had desired, but not really imagined. I had invested wisely in a real estate portfolio and built my net worth to over a million dollars. I was respected professionally in the automobile industry. I had come so far from that day on Derby Street when I was embarrassed to use food stamps. I continually met and exceeded expectations in the workplace, and even with an initial naivete about inter-office maneuvering, I was promoted to progressively responsible leadership roles every few years. I had graduated from college with honors and was working on an M.B.A. I had traveled most of the United States, and abroad to Europe, Paris, Jamaica, Bahamas, Mexico, the Cayman Islands and more. Additionally, I had experienced starkly different cultures in the different places I had lived. In many ways, I was a woman of the world.

But there was a part of me that was not present in the executive suites I moved in every day. Something I unknowingly hide safely away from everyone. I was social, approachable and friendly – but I never truly let people get close enough to get to know me really. At some level, I guess I just didn't trust. It felt safe. I felt like if I remained guarded no letting anyone penetrate, they couldn't reject or disapprove of me...the real, inner me. No one could hurt the little girl behind the professional exterior if they never got close to her. Despite everything I had achieved, I still feared that the real me" was not -- good enough, special enough, established enough, accepted enough --- and I feared public security would destroy me because I was the only one who could truly "protect me."

This professional prison in which I lived "worked: in a manner of speaking" for many years. Working in a male-dominated industry, I experienced many "isms" – sexism, racism, etc. but succeeded by not letting that narrative define or stop me. The image I projected, at least from my point of view, was purely professional. I simply did not accept at the time that my race and sex, though part of me, were part of that image I intentionally displayed. While the "front" prevented others from knowing the real me, which was the effect I desired at the time, it also hurt me and didn't allow me to grow personally. And this became even more important. The wall I had built between my real self and the rest of the world also kept me in. It prevented me from stepping outside myself, and made me blind to what was around me...what I really looked like.

As a rape survivor, I consciously avoided projecting my sexuality. I only wanted to be seen as a professional. The flaw in this plan was that everyone else saw me as a woman and as an African American, in a male-dominated industry, who happened to be a professional—in that order. The more I tried this tactic of presenting myself as sexless and race-less, the less effective it was. In retrospect it makes sense. I was denying aspects of myself that every human has. A reasonable observer might ask, "If you have no sex and no race, then what are you? Because you're not like any person I've ever seen."

I came to understand that many challenges I faced professionally were likely the result of people perceiving something disingenuous in me – an unseen layer. I appeared to be hiding something. And I was. I was masking a part of me. And as successful as I was, I could never reach my full potential until I could use my full power as a woman. In truth, I was still a little girl inside, and I would not risk hurting her by exposing her to the ills of the world and the challenges of the workplace. I wanted to keep her innocent and pure. But that would never work, because I was no longer a little girl, and the rest of the world knew that, perhaps better than I did.

With few exceptions, all I had ever known, seen, or experienced from men was exploitation and abuse. My stepfather and the rapist, these were the dominant male images in my mind. I sensed that in every male I came into contact with, and the result was that it generated fear and anger within me. In an industry dominated by men, I was in somewhat personal distress. This was not a good formula for long-term success.

Professionally, I thought I had it made. But I still had no plan for my life beyond work. I just reached out for whatever was in front of me, be it a promotion or the successful completion of one project at a time. Like I said, "Success by accident." It was like I was driving a car at night, and could only see a hundred feet in front of my headlights. Eventually, I got somewhere, but I didn't know where that was going to be until I got there. Eventually, I began to realize that personally, I needed more. In fact, I really had no real personal life.

I was married on March 31, 2008. I was introduced to him by a colleague at work. The man I married was made in the image of the men in my childhood. He was physically, verbally, and psychologically abusive. He was unfaithful. But he was worse than my father, or my stepfather, because he was a functional alcoholic. This made him not only violent, but unpredictable. I lived in fear and learned to walk on eggshells throughout the marriage because I never knew what he was going to do, or how bad it would be.

The relationship with my husband made things at work much worse. My husband was a project manager, and I was a director, a senior executive. He resented my level of authority, and he resented my success, especially my financial success. He spent a great deal of my wealth on drunken escapades and his affairs with other women. But in addition to that, he also spoke ill of me at work – among our friends, even though my success at work was the source of his spending money. He would downplay my achievements in front of me and behind my back. He was aggressive and physically abusive, and once knocked me across a kitchen floor in front of his mother, and his youngest son.

I had always wondered why my mother kept allowing Tharmond to come back, time after time. I probably told myself that if a man was unfaithful to me, that would be the end. But one day I was sitting with him at his computer. We were ordering something online. While I was watching, he received an instant message from a woman. It said, "I love you, I miss you, and I can't wait to be with you again." I said nothing. My heart sank. My entire body felt numb. I had fallen into the same trap my mother had. As bad as things were, living with an abusive alcoholic, this seemed like the worst thing possible at that moment. Of course, my husband tried to pretend it was just a joke, but he eventually admitted he was having an affair. Later, I found out he had been with dozens of women while we were married, including some that claimed to be my friends.

Nothing in my life had prepared me for the devastation I felt as my marriage crumbled before my eyes. I had never been unfaithful to my husband, and never would be, even after I discovered his affairs. I had made my choice when I married him, and I was responsible for the consequences of that choice. To cheat, to me, even in light of his unfaithfulness, would betray weakness in my own character.

The crazy thing was I still believed that the marriage could be saved and that I needed to do what I could to save it. My husband agreed, and we went to counseling together. But he eventually stopped going. He wanted nothing to do with me, the abusive behavior in a way, was his way of getting me to leave. We separated in 2010. In the end, he was the one who decided to end the marriage. For whatever reason, I didn't. The full extent of his deception would only become known to me years later. My husband, said our therapist, was a narcissist, in addition to being an alcoholic. Unless he got help, he would always see the others around him as a threat, a problem. He would continue to manipulate and abuse them as he had been doing. And he was an exceptionally good manipulator. He was charming. My marriage had been a swindle, for my money, and for someone to blame for all his troubles and insecurities.

Years later, I learned from his mother that my husband had targeted me specifically for what he felt I had. My condominium, my money – things I had worked hard to acquire. He stayed with me, even when he knew it was not working, specifically to use me for my money and lifestyle. And while we were married, he promised another woman that he would marry her, telling her that he only married me because I had a terminal illness, and he could not leave me, but that when I was gone, they would marry. Finally, he divorced me. When he had spent all of my money, he no longer had any use for me and needed to find a new host to support his parasitic lifestyle. The depths of this deception sickened me. But knowing the truth did not help me put together a plan for my life. For that, I didn't know how nor where to get the inspiration.

CHAPTER 9:

HITTING BOTTOM

A lcoholics refer to a *bottom* as the point in life when things get so bad that a change for the better is forced, and there is no place to go but up. At this point in my life, I felt like I was at that low point. The failure of my marriage was one contributor to this. In a way, I was fortunate because my husband's sickness drove him away before he did more damage. But he had done quite a bit of damage already. He continually told me that I was a problem, a failure, and a fake at work, and that everyone but me knew it. His continual mental abuse had me believing I was insane and not fit for my job. In this state of mind and with him still working there, I negotiated a severance package and left Harley-Davidson.

I believed the things I was told about myself. I assumed that my husband loved me and would not tell me things that were not true. I already felt alone in my marriage, fearful of what my husband might do or say. And I had decided not to be unfaithful. I was alone, and now I did not even have a job to go to. I felt completely isolated and worthless. I began to have thoughts of ending my life.

I had a failed suicide attempt as a teenager, but this time was different. I have described my attempted suicide at age sixteen, and I think that was really a cry for help, for escape from the general abuse and dysfunction that plagued my household when I was growing up. As an adult in the kind of marriage I was in, I felt an enormous, gut-wrenching pain in every part of me. It was not a reaction to things happening around me. It was an internal pain, and there was so much of it. Emotionally, physically, and psychologically, I was hurting. And I thought I was the problem. I thought I was the source of my own pain.

Fortunately, out there. I had friends. One of them called me, seemingly out of the blue. We talked and caught up with each other's lives. He was at the National Association of Automobile Dealers (NADA) convention in New Orleans. Like any good friend, he knew by the sound of my voice that something was terribly wrong. He wanted to help, and he was not going to let me sit there in pain. So he invited me to visit and even got me a room and a ticket to New Orleans.

It was after Hurricane Katrina had hit, and there was much work to be done in the city, but it was still New Orleans, and I had always enjoyed being there. I think it also did me good simply to be somewhere else. In Milwaukee, my condominium, the city, all of the things around me were a reminder of how bad my life was. My whole being cried out for escape. I had been thinking of escaping by suicide. But this friend had now provided a far more healthy escape.

I found out that I had other friends in New Orleans at the time, which I had worked with in the industry. One night, I went to lunch with my friend Dora. I had known her when we both worked at Harley-Davidson. We went to Café du Monde, and had a good time catching up with each other.

Sometime before lunch, I looked up and noticed a street performer nearby. It was a black man, with specks of grey in his beard and his sparse remaining hair. He was sitting down, playing saxophone and accompanying himself with drums and cymbals that he played with his feet. For some reason I do not understand, I could not take my eyes off of him. And he looked back at me. He smiled and played. As he played, I heard the sound you hear when a needle scratches an old vinyl record. In that instant, he began to play *This Little Light of Mine.*, like a message designated for me ready to play, collecting dust on a shelf while my life fell apart. And I heard the song play; I heard a voice inside me, saying:

I put this light inside you and no one
not even you,
has the right to put it out.

I was taken by surprise. I know this was a spiritual experience if I have ever had one. The voice I was hearing was strong and intense, but at the same time comforting. It made me feel as if there was nothing wrong with me, that I was perfectly designed and beautiful and good. It was inside me, but at the same time, I knew it was something bigger than I was. Someone or something that loved me more than any man or woman ever could.

I spent the remainder of my time in New Orleans reflecting on my life and the world. I looked at the destruction around me, and it reminded me of my life. The hurt and disappointment I had endured was like the destruction wreaked by this enormous force of nature, the hurricane. The floods were like all of the tears I had shed over my marriage. The displaced people were like my hope and love and happiness--emptied somewhere else. And like this city, I now really had only one option. The thoughts of ending my life were behind me since I had re-discovered a light inside of me that no one could extinguish. So the only way forward was to rebuild. And this time, I would be looking to what had been there all along, the light inside me. In that moment, I didn't know how but I knew this time I would be *Betting On Me*.

CHAPTER 10:

COMMUNITY

H e lifted me out of the slimy pit, out of the mud and mire;
he set my feet on a rock and gave me a firm place to stand.
Psalm 40:2

Humans are communal people. We naturally gravitate to
each other and form communities. This dynamic includes competition, compassion, altruism – even the individualist is de-
fined by his apartness from the community. So it makes sense
that our communities form us. And most of us have a number
of communities in our lives. Coworkers, superiors, and subor-

dinates form our work community. The family is another group of communities. Our churches, schools, charities, and sports teams all are groups of people living, working, playing or praying in community. This is why as we grow and develop in the different areas of our lives, the growth does not happen evenly. One may grow more as leader in her community softball league. One may grow more intellectually in a book club. And sometimes a community doesn't provide any growth at all. The effect can be negative as well.

I learned to grow as a business leader because the communities in the companies and industries in which I worked helped me grow, sometimes by competition, sometimes by encouragement and guidance. But my private life did not provide this kind of positive growth environment for many years. I had very little guidance and encouragement. It took difficult events to break me down so that I could begin building a personal life that would match my business success.

CHAPTER 11:

ENLIGHTENMENT

In 2010 I left an abusive marriage. I left a successful career. I had lost all of my wealth and assets I had acquired prior to the marriage. Things were ending for me, and things were beginning as well because I had learned one very important thing. The spark of my life did not come from betting on family, friends, career or others. It was inside me. I just had to draw my inspiration from that source. The universal source that gave me life. I had lost so much. I felt as if I had nothing else to lose-which made it as good a time as any to "bet on me."

It was not an easy time for me. In fact, this was the most challenging time of my life. Despite the successes I had had in business up until that point, I needed very much to work. It was an economically challenging time for many people, especially me. The period now referred to as the Great Recession of 2008, was in full effect. Though the recession technically ended in 2010, there was little to no real growth for years afterward. Businesses were laying off thousands while I was trying to start a consulting business and build a client list.

The business I started in Milwaukee in 2009 was a consulting firm called Cultural-Nuances. It focused on the cultural aspects of operational business strategy and planning- the business case for doing business with diverse populations. It was formed to help businesses optimize effectiveness, utilization, and performance of a diverse workforce, and to do this with an understanding of the cultural environment of the workforce. I wanted to leverage my business education, cultural marketing experience from the automotive industry, my six sigma green belt certification, and my outreach marketing communication expertise from the Powersports industry to help companies understand cultural impact and influence in the marketplace.

Unfortunately, it was very hard trying to build a new business from scratch at this time-especially without an anchor client. Especially as marketing organizations, in particular, were hard hit by the downturn. And although the business hobbled along, it was not enough for me to survive on. A contact from my automotive days helped me get a job interview and job as a field marketing manager in the financial services industry. It allowed me a way out of my current financial dilemma and exit strategy out of the nightmare that was my marriage. Later, I had an opportunity to relocate to Arizona, and assume responsibilities in the western region of the company. After having been a senior level executive at two fortune 100 companies, it was a significant step-down. But it brought in much-needed income. Everything was so different. It was very humbling and having fewer responsibilities in life was probably what I needed at that time. I desperately needed work to bring in income. Everything in my life was crumbling around me. One by one lost each investment property, assets and valuable I had owned. What was going on? How had it come to this? I continued doing them be as productive as possible on the job. While I did my best to stay low key, perform my duties and not create any waves, I felt so fragile. During the day, I managed to perform my duties. At night, I had difficulties talking, trusting, believing, and relating to anyone. At work, people seemed to be threatened by me. Or at least that is how it seemed. I was not aggressively trying to advance as I just wanted, needed to make money to survive. I infused the knowledge of my experience into my work. As a former marketing director doing the role of a field manager, naturally I had experience beyond that of my peers. I did not desire to rock the boat, merely bring home a paycheck. I was tapped to take on additional territory when a colleague went out on maternity leave. Going into that market, I did things similar to the way I did them in my territory, but I guess it was somewhat beyond what the colleague responsible for that area did. I did nothing to know that, nor was I trying to overshadow her.

I just wanted to do my job. When she returned, she was brutal because she thought I wanted her territory or that I was deliberately trying to make her look bad. I had a carousel of young managers. Again I just wanted to coast and bring home a paycheck. They were trying to excel, make a name for themselves. I had seen it, been it, and done it. I felt stifled and constantly looking over my back or pulling daggers out of my back from the backstabbing. I didn't want this. It hurt.

On and off during that time I never stopped trying to secure an anchor client for my business. I worked eight hours at the job then worked for myself when I got home. I did not give up. I believed in my dream of having a successful small business. Success was not forthcoming or easy. I still needed a day job.

In 2013, the financial services company I worked for reorganized and centralized the field marketing division to their headquarter in Madison, Wisconsin. I cringed at the notion of going back there and felt a toxic sickening at the thought of going back. The thought of living in Wisconsin and all the things that had happened there-things that made me want to give up on life. I couldn't do it. I would die-literally. I respectfully declined the move-which made my manager happy. It was a bold move for me. Opting to give up regular income, knowing how difficult it might be to find another job since the country had not fully recovered from the economic downturn. But I desperately felt I needed to take care of me.

There was another reason I did not go back to Wisconsin. Ever since that day in New Orleans, I would think about the voice I heard when that musician played "This Little Light of

Mine." *I put this light inside you and no one, not even you, has the right to put it out.* My life would not be driven by others, even if it meant leaving a job. After years of climbing the corporate ladder and building a business portfolio, I finally realized -- I am not my job, and I am not the company I work for. I am worth betting on because of that spark inside me that was made to shine for a specific purpose. And the spark will never go out. I was scared but felt good about the decision to stay in Phoenix, but I realized betting on me was not going to be easy. With everything I had gone through, I felt the real difficulty was not in going or not going to Wisconsin, but rather, I would be settling and more importantly -- not living my purpose.

Since arriving in Arizona, I had lived in a condominium that I really loved, but in deciding not to relocate and the extended amount time is taking to find work, it was more than I felt I could afford. I wound up moving in with a friend in lieu of living in my car. I could not believe the turn my life had taken. I had been a millionaire just a few years earlier, with a six-hundred-thousand-dollar condominium overlooking the river, investment properties around the country, a senior executive job. Now I was renting a room. I was humbled and grateful.

The living situation was uncomfortable for me in other ways as well. The man renting the room to me had child custody problems and problems with women that he dated. And for some reason, as hard as I tried not to be involved in these problems, he would pull me into them. However, I am grateful that he gave me the opportunity to live there for a while when I really needed that.

Eventually, my friend's financial situation got worse, and he needed more money for the room I was renting from him. Financially, it no longer made sense for me to stay there. My consulting business had picked up some. I also found work with another friend at a startup business, marketing electric cars for a company in California called EcoCentre. With the income from this job and my own consulting fees, I was more financially stable and able to move into a small townhouse. My life was finally starting to stabilize in a good way. But I wanted more fulfillment in my vocation. Dr. Sahney had taught me not to settle, and he taught me well.

Getting back on my feet, then moving forward was a long process. And it was fraught with frustration along the way. While I worked a job during the day and built my business at night, I was also dealing with the carnage of my former marriage, and just kept putting off the hard task of salvaging what I had. I would be paying off those debts for a long time. Counseling made things better, especially when I learned the true depths of my husband's deception. But I had more setbacks. A couple of months after I moved into the townhouse, a storm caused the roof to cave in through two floors. The kitchen roof almost fell on top of me, missing by only seconds! After that, there was a wall-to-wall pool of water, four inches deep, on the main level of my home. The damage took months to repair. To make things worse, my landlord was not sympathetic to my plight, and I suspected the building structure had been compromised before the storm occurred. The thing I realized during that time was I had a remarkable calmness and patience in my spirit that I had never really noticed before. In how I responded, handled and faced things during that time. I was transforming on the inside, as I continued to heal, and it was coming through in how I dealt with people and things in my life. Like I had learned that life was happening *for* me, not to me.

The job at EcoCentre was enough to get me by, but it was not enough money. However, as I continued to work, I also continued and would continue to strive to build my business concurrently. I poured every extra penny into my consulting firm, which would become Austin Group Consulting. I also served on the boards of several charities. This did not only helped me to give back to the community, but it allowed me to build relationships in Phoenix, a place where a few years back I had arrived with a one-way ticket from Wisconsin, a suitcase packed for 2 weeks, knowing no one. In many ways, I needed those relationships as much as they needed the value of the experience I brought to the table. We all need relationships to thrive. None of us can succeed in life alone.

In 2015 I began working in a marketing role for a wealth management firm. It was a job, and provided more income stability. But every day I would still go home from this job and work hours on *my* business. From the beginning, I knew I could provide value to the employer, but that it was not a "life-long" job. I desired that I might be able to turn my employer into a client eventually. This is an example of action on the enlightenment I have found. It's about believing in myself, my business, and not depending on the beliefs of others. I still need a paycheck, but more than anything, I want to pay myself!

The employer's vision and my vision at one point didn't align on the same track. While the pay and benefits were quite helpful, the employer was big on titles and perception of status to outsiders, while internally, he really only wanted an executive assistant. Occasionally, it also appeared as if he didn't want me to have my own identity. It seemed as if he was insecure or felt threatened by me -- because I served on City committees, attended functions with the Mayor, Governor, elected officials, etc. From my vantage point, these were seeds I had sown after arriving in Phoenix, and I was reaping benefits of work I had performed. It felt stifling. I could not breathe. I could hear the high school counselor's voice *"the most you can expect to be is a secretary,"* every time he would ask me to get coffee, make cappuccino, pick up the clients from the waiting room. I did it and I didn't complain, but everything inside of me was screaming, yelling, kicking, and fighting. I think it was so blatantly difficult for me because of my journey, but mostly because I knew this was not my purpose. I love all aspects of the marketing communications discipline, but I had absolutely no passion, desire or interest in financial services marketing in this manner. I strived to deliver on the promises I made to him, but eventually, I knew I had severely outgrown being able to be the beneficial contributor he needed, desired and deserved. I advised that instead of looking for a marketing director, it might better serve his needs in hiring a highly-qualified executive assistant, with insurance licensing and interest in serving him in the way he needed, wanted and desired. I completed the assignments I had been working on and decided -- once again -- to bet on me.

The summer after leaving this job, I felt freer than I had - ever. I wasn't making much income but had time to work on my business strategy, take meetings, network, and plan. I continued to engage in the community, serve and support the organizations I was involved. I learned there was a huge teacher shortage, so I got a K-12 substitute and specialized business and marketing teaching certificate. I taught all grades, but definitely had a preference for older students.

Where I needed additional income, I drove for several car transportation services. In between business activities, I would drive. I put a lot of miles on my car, but I had time to think, plan, work and money to pay bills.

One day, I received an email from Grand Canyon University asking for additional information about an adjunct position that was available. I optimistically responded. I had always wanted to teach at a university - after I retired. It was a part of my long-term plan. I could never have imagined the path I took as the road to teaching at a university, but as life would have it -- this was my journey.

I later got a call for an interview. The interview process was amazing. It was the first time in so many years that I felt valued, appreciated and wanted professionally. It was refreshing, uplifting and invigorating. I started teaching Marketing 415, two nights a week. There was something magical in how it felt to teach at the university level. How I poured into the students from my experiences and how great it made me feel to see "the light bulb come on" for students as they got or understood a concept I had presented. In every job I had ever had, I was

-- in many ways-- an instructor of sorts, but this was something special. The feeling made Betting On Me, make sense - it was The BOM!

CHAPTER 12:

INTEGRATION

When I say, I'm The BOM. I generally wait a moment to allow people to take in what I have said and form an impression. The look on people's faces is usually somewhere between "did I hear what I think I heard," or "Wow, she's full of herself," but as I explain it, they understand and agree. Being The BOM does not mean being self-centered or self-focused. It means being self-propelled. It means living your purpose. Even while struggling financially I worked on charity boards, spoke to domestic violence and at-risk teens, and participated in local politics. I was applying the concept of The BOM: Using every experience life had given me and packaging to work for me– toward living my purpose.

Initially speaking with domestic violence or at-risk teen groups terrified me – when I thought about the story I would share about my life, my beginnings, and my rises and falls – it would leave me completely drained. But eventually, speaking with them energized me. I have been through so much that I knew anything they took to heart would pay dividends for them in the long run, and would plant a seed in them that could lead to a better life for themselves. It also exposed me to something that would change my life--helping others succeed personally in life. Business consulting is one thing, something that comes easily to me due to my long experience as an executive. I was to discover that teaching, personal development coaching, and writing would also be a significant part of my future -- and living my purpose.

While I looked for work and for clients, I had a strange difficulty. Looking younger is usually not seen as a problem. Many people would like to look younger than they are. But I looked like I was in my thirties, while I was in my fifties. I think people looked at me and did not believe that I had enough experience to do the job or provide the service they needed. It took some real effort to get past that.

I decided that if I was going to Bet on Me, then it was important to improve myself. Even though I had a wealth of experience and two business degrees, I needed to branch out and continue to build on my strengths. Although I had been an avid reader of motivational and success books for many years, I had not had the insight I now possessed. It was time to apply my knowledge to a life in which I was, as my grandmother would say, prepared for the opportunity -- Betting On Me. One of the ways I did this was to get involved in coaching. I believe to be a complete person we must teach and help others, and this helped me to be better at helping others. I set a goal to become a published author, and I started writing. TheBOM, this book, is my fourth book and I plan to continue writing as long as I have something to say that can help someone else. You can see a list of my other books at the front of this book!

It was important for me to Bet on Me in my personal life as well as my professional life. When I moved to Arizona, I thought it was important to take a step back from dating for a while after my divorce. I felt like I needed to stabilize myself before adding a new aspect to my life. Also, I didn't want to go into another relationship, hurt, bitter and angry. The stereotype of an "angry black woman" who had been hurt in a relationship. I also felt that "hurt people, hurt people." I knew I was hurt; I didn't want to hurt anyone else, so I took the time to heal. Then my professional life took precedence for a while. I have always been a hard worker, another reason for my success in light of daunting obstacles. But I also feel that I need balance in my life, to not be the professional front while hiding the little girl inside me...I needed to allow her to grow up – to mature. So I occasionally go out on dates – not dating per se, but an occasional date. So far, I do not have anyone in particular that is special. But I already know that when it happens, it will be special. He will not seek to define, or control who I am. Rather he will accept, cherish and respect who I am. I have come to know who I am. My special man will be a complement to my own brilliant little light.

CHAPTER 13:

FREEDOM

At this point in life, Betting On Me is reflective of planting seeds in building a business that will provide me independence from working as an employee. I have speaking engagements in which I talk about how Betting On Me has turned my life around. I share my story with others. I have a freedom now which gives me the strength to give generously in whatever way I can.

I continue my charity work, because I know I always receive ten times what I give away. I have served on charitable board throughout most of my adult life so serving on Phoenix-area boards and committees was no exception. One example is Florence Crittenton's Inspire Program, a mentoring forum in which we hold panel discussions for teens, provide inspirational stories, insight, and personal testimonies. We don't just share a "rags to riches" story. We share insight on the peaks and valleys, the struggle and the insight. The concept of TheBOM came out of these sessions. Back in 2013, when I had an ah-ha moment of discovery. I had the book title that would take three more years before I would actually begin to write. I really love sharing my Betting On Me philosophy with these young ladies whenever I get the opportunity.

I am a published author and continue to write books that teach, inspire and spread a positive message of empowerment and love. I write books because I know it will allow me to reach many times the number of people I could ever personally meet or even speak to at one of my engagements. I look forward to hearing from anyone who has been impacted by my books and to reading their stories of how Betting On Me worked in their lives.

I am a motivational speaker, and my speaking engagements and fees continue to increase. While I cannot reach as many people as I can through my books, I get to meet people face to face, and this is more rewarding on a personal level.

Sometimes I can help someone with an instant inspiration, other times it takes time. But seeing the positive difference in the faces of the audience members feeds back into my own confidence. Because having an impact on others is *my* goal.

I am a personal success coach, helping others to create the lives they have always dreamed of and to reach their full potential. An even more personal and individual level of interaction, this is perhaps the most rewarding work that I do. I want my experience to help others, not just by inspiring them, but by helping them to recognize their own inner light, and by this enlightenment, to self-power them to even more success than I have achieved in their lives.

I am an adjunct professor, guiding, inspiring and teaching marketing, advertising, promotions as well as consumer and buyer behavior. Grand Canyon University is a Christian university, and I love that I can also integrate faith and Christian values into the teaching experience for my students.

I love hearing stories of people I have impacted through my books, talks, and coaching. This is my true desire and my true joy. I Bet On Me and won the jackpot. It is making a difference in the lives of others.

Betting On Me has made all the difference in my life. Everything I needed was inside me all along. Seeds have been planted. Others have helped and hurt along the way. I place no blame for my life on those who have hurt me, and I thank those who have helped. Along the way, the seeds that have been planted were sometimes fertilized by encouragement, sometimes scorched or mishandled as in bad weather, by loneliness. But when it was time, and the one choice I had was me, everything everyone had sown into me over the years – the things that built character and strength, the things that made me laugh and made me cry – all of those things came to life when I decided to bet on me. Everything that has happened *to* me has happened *for* me. No one has made more of an impact on my success than the motivation, the inspiration, and the determination of the light that burns inside of me. I hope that you make the same discovery about yourself. In the next part, I'll outline how you can achieve your own success and find your own inner light.

CHAPTER 14:

PERIPHERAL VISION

For the revelation awaits an appointed time; it speaks of the end and will not prove false. Though it lingers, wait for it; it will certainly come and will not delay. Habakkuk 2:3

I have a plan for you! It is relatively simple. But it is not easy. It takes hard work. For me, hard work was never the problem. The problem was developing a plan. I did what I call "succeeding by accident." I worked hard, I tightened my grip, and things eventually got somewhere good. It works for a particular project, but it is not a strategy for life. In life, I needed to have a plan. I did not necessarily need to know everything that was going to happen for the rest of my life – that is impossible. But I needed a plan to find out where I was going.

I have taken a few driver safety courses. In these courses, drivers learn how to be vigilant, patient, and cautious on the road. One way to do this is to use your peripheral vision. Your central vision should be focused on the horizon, so you can see things happening directly in front of you a long time before you have to act on them. In this way, you have plenty of time and can take safe action to avoid trouble.

The same concept applies to living a successful and fulfilled life. The end goal may change, just as it changes when you are driving and take a turn. But it is not about avoiding trouble—it is about visualizing achievement. And you are always looking ahead—way ahead, all the way to the horizon--and making adjustments to get where you are going.

This part of the book outlines my plan for you. I will summarize it briefly here, and then we'll get down to business:

1. Have an Attitude for Thinking: Prepare your mind to lead you to great things and avoid the pitfalls that can keep you from reaching your vision.

2. Plan for Success: Look at the horizon, but see your vision, not someone else's. You must have a destination in order to reach it.

3. Understand and Use Attraction To Reach Your Goals: Knowing this time-honored principle and using it to guide your thoughts is essential to achieving things seemingly beyond your grasp.

4. Wake Up and Take Action: Find the energy and stamina to do what no coach or author can do for you—the hard work that leads to your vision.

5. Be Accountable: Believe that you are in control of your own life. Take responsibility and hold yourself accountable, so you continue to progress toward your vision.

6. Be Persistent and Persevere: Learn how to never give up before reaching your goal.

Now turn the page and let's get started!

Lynn F. Austin

CHAPTER 15:

HAVE AN ATTITUDE FOR THINKING

For every step in this process, be aware that there is a negative side and a positive side. It is important to have positive paradigms on which you will depend for self-motivation, but you must also be aware of the negative paradigms that can take away your motivation to succeed. As Jack Canfield says in his book *The Success Principles*, "It's not what you don't know that holds you back. It's what you do know that isn't true." This is how powerful negative thoughts, which are often deeply ingrained within us, can be.

Expect to win. I expect to win, and I keep expecting to win, and I expect to keep winning. That is my mantra. It isn't enough to survive; I expect to thrive. My plan does not include failure. It simply is not in my playbook.

Be-Do-Have, not Have-Do-Be. Be-Do-Have is a concept elaborated by Natalie Ledwell and others that you should take to heart. There is a common fallacy that in order to be a specific something, you need to do a specific something, and in order to do that something, you need to have a specific something. It is the reverse of The Be-Do-Have principle. This idea is best explained using examples:

Lacking (Have-Do-Be): I need lots of money, so I can buy a BMW. I need to *have* the BMW so I can drive to work in it and be seen driving to work in it and parking in the company parking lot. I need to *do* this so I can *be* confident at work.

Abundant (Be-Do-Have): I have everything I need inside of me. I am betting on me because of that. I am what I need to *be*. Because of this, I *do* only what leads me to success. And I *can* do it. Because of this, I *have* whatever I need, whether it is a BMW or a Rolls Royce or a jumbo mining dump truck to carry my money to the bank.

The reverse concept is what you probably see and hear every day in commercials on radio and television. If you have this razor with all its capabilities, you will be able to meet beautiful women have them around you. If you have this car, you will be able to better care for your family and will have a more wholesome life. If you have this shampoo, you will be able to shake your hair loose and dazzle every man in the room. It is the American way or one version of it.

This false idea is now embedded in our culture. Every business person knows they need to fill a need in order to sell something to a lot of people. In advertising, the goal is to *create* the need in the mind of the consumer. People buy things not because they want the things themselves, but because they want what they think these things will bring them. People buy certain cars because they think they will be more powerful if they have that car. They do not admit this, even to themselves, but it is true nonetheless.

This concept may work from an advertising perspective. But from a personal point of view, it is a problem. It conflicts with the Law of Attraction, a time-proven concept which I will discuss in Chapter 15. The advertising strategy is a step backward, not a step forward. Have-do-be requires you first to envision a need. You cannot start until you have something, and you don't have it because you aren't what you want to be. It focuses on lack, deficiency, what is missing.

To achieve your goal, you need to live a life of abundance. If you are not good enough, you'll do what is not good enough and have what is not good enough. But if you are everything you need to be, if you are complete, then what you can do and have are infinite. There are no limits. So start from a place of abundance (be). Take action and work hard (do). Then you will have everything you desire.

* * * *

In addition to expecting to win, and being in a state of abundance, it is important to align your feelings with what you want. This is part of the attitude you must live with to get progressively closer to your goal. In the next chapter, you will learn the importance of defining what you want. What are the emotions you experience when you have what you want? Bring these to mind and let them occur in your body. Feel the emotions of having your ideal mate, home, job, and impact on the world. Get familiar with these feelings and encourage them on a daily basis.

Your attitude for living will define what the future holds for you. Start with these attitudes, and they will begin to affect not just your goals, but your daily life. In your life, things will happen by surprise. You won't necessarily be expecting or planning them, but if you are armed with attitudes of abundance, expectation of success, and an emotional state of satisfaction and joy, you may surprise yourself at how well you deal with life's surprises.

CHAPTER 16:

PLAN FOR LIFE SUCCESS

In my life, I thought I had a plan for success in business. It brought me success, so I thought it was working. And it did, in a way. But as I look at my early business career I can see that it was based on *success by accident*. My success was less about a plan but more about just working hard to get things done. And the only thing I got done was the project in front of me. These projects, the various jobs I had, none of them were leading to anything else. I worked on them as stand-alone projects. As a result, my life did not progress in a way that gave me any kind of satisfaction. Remember the driver safety courses I mentioned at the beginning of this part? Imagine driving a car and only thinking about the car in front of you or the next turn, and not your destination. You would never get there. That is what it is like to live your life without a plan. That is success by accident.

I thought I had a foolproof plan for succeeding in every project I accepted. I thought I could run on autopilot. I ignored the bigger picture of my life and career. So I succeeded by accident for many years. Now what I have been discussing here refers to my professional life. I tried to keep that my only life. I wanted everyone at work to see the professional me and not the whole me. My personal life, to a point, had been non-existent. I would uproot myself and go wherever I was told to get the next promotion, leaving behind my living environment, friends, and activities. I simply disregarded that part of my life as not important enough to have a say it what happened to me. After years of this, I got married, and the result was a lot of damage to my mind, body, soul, and fortune. Any plan for success, for life, must include a *whole* life.

So how do you find a plan for your life? It has to start with knowing what you want. If you cannot envision the destination, you will never reach it. If you determine what you want and keep your focus on this, it will be impossible *not* to succeed in getting there. You will be drawn to it. Your actions will inevitably take you there. More importantly, everything you need to accomplish your goal will be drawn to you. Can you see how this reinforces the concept of abundance discussed in the last chapter? You already have what you need. In order to draw these things to you, you only need to envision the end goal that requires them.

If you start out with little encouragement and even a good measure of discouragement, like I did, it may be difficult to figure out what you want. You may unintentionally limit your choices. Be aware of these and dare to dream. The most common problem people have with this step is dreaming too small, only seeing things that are already around them. But if that is the limit of your vision, you will only wind up with more of the same. What you have is what you will always have. That is *not* the case for you. Dream huge.

You may already know what you want, and your definition may be very specific. But if you are not sure, here are some ideas that may help you to get there. This process will also help you ensure that you are not artificially limiting yourself.

First, take a look at several areas of your life and imagine how you want them to be. Forget how the world is now. Forget your job and any crises and stresses you are now experiencing. Imagine that the world is perfect and you can have whatever you want. There are no limitations on you. What does it look like? Remember, no one but you can decide your future. Think of this as a movie in which you are the writer, director, and star. You call the shots, you create the characters and the sets, and decide how it begins and ends. But this is not a fictional story; it is a true one – a documentary about your future!

Finances.

For many people, this is the most important concern, because it leads to and from so many other things. But for now, let's set it aside. We want to define the things and situations it leads to and from first.

Health.

How do you feel in this no-limits world? Are you ready to run a marathon? Are you built like a champion bodybuilder or a world-class gymnast? Or are you simply free of disease, taking no medication, and determined to keep it that way? Is your mind clear, powerful and getting stronger? Are you going to live a long, full life? What age will you live to be?

Now refine this vision. How much do you weigh? How good is your eyesight? How fast can you run or walk a mile? What does your doctor say to you when you have a checkup?

Home.

Where do you live? What does the surrounding landscape or cityscape look like? Are the spaces expansive and airy, or compact and cozy? Are you in an RV with a few days' supply of water, or living in a mountain cabin by a rushing stream? What is the climate like? Can you look out on the beach from your living room, and wear shorts year-round? Can you step out of your door into a dizzying array of New England leaves in autumn? Are you living in a desert in a Bedouin-style tent and ready to move in few days, on to the next adventure on horseback or camelback?

As you further define your vision, think about the things in and around your home. Is there a pool? Or a porch or deck overlooking a lush Montana valley? What kind of furniture do you have? Is there a home theatre? What do you watch there, and with whom? Is there a library with paneling and lush leather chairs where you read your favorite authors and ponder philosophical topics? Or will you spend time in your own home gym, complete with a world-renown trainer? Are there many guest rooms where you may entertain people from all walks of life? Is there a chapel for meditation and prayer?

Relationship.

What does your family look like? What about your social life? Are you a loving and dedicated spouse or parent, or both? Do you have twenty adopted children aged two to twenty-two? Is your front door a revolving door for a large group of extended family and friends? Do you have dinner parties or attend them every week? Or do you enjoy a few very close friendships and relationships and a life of relative quiet?

Who is your ideal mate? Imagine this person in detail, including hair color, facial characteristics, body type. What are the names of your children? What activities do you share with your closest friend? What do you serve at those dinner parties or sports game get-togethers?

Career.

What sort of work environment are you in? Are you an independently wealthy full-time philanthropist? Do you run your own business? Do you work for a church or charity? Who are your coworkers? Describe the perfect boss. Why do you work? What drives you? What is your workplace like, physically? Imagine a perfect workplace in which you enjoy the entire work day. Is there music? Are there computers, or do you spend a lot of time on your feet or meeting with people to make plans? Is it outdoors? Or on a ship or boat? An archeological dig in the Middle East? Remember, there are no limits. This is your dream.

Bring this vision into focus. What is the name of your company? What does the logo look like? How many hours do you work? What color is the carpet or floor of your office? Get as much detail as possible into your description.

Finally, Finances. You have described the type of life you want to live. But not how you are going to pay for it. Don't worry about it! In fact, forget about it. If you focus on your dream, the money will take care of itself. Most people think of financial position in terms of the kind of lifestyle they want to live. So imagine what kind of car you want to drive or be driven in, where you want to live and what kind of house, apartment, condominium, cabin, RV, boat, or whatever else you can think of might be your dwelling.

Be detailed. What make and model of sports car or luxury sedan do you have? What is your driver's name? What about your tailor or dress designer? What brand of watch do you wear? Do you prefer diamonds or pearls?

It is not important to be concerned about how these things will come to you at this point. It is extremely important to clarify your vision. Spend time thinking about your dream. Personally, I like to meditate on my vision right after I get in bed, before I go to sleep. It is a good way to relax, and there is usually enough quiet at that point to allow me to concentrate. Define your dream and continue to think about the details. Develop a picture in your mind that you can see at any time. If someone asks you where you want to be, you should be able to describe it in intricate detail.

And it is a good idea to do just that. Whether or not you have a friend or relative that shares your type of vision, it is important to vocalize it to someone who will be open and supportive. Many of us had parents who tried to play down our dreams in hopes of making us more pragmatic. It isn't their fault. They want to shield us from disappointment and in fact, it is a parent's job to prepare children to survive in the real world.

But we want to do more than survive; we want to thrive. So if your parent is like that, it would be better not to share this dream with him or her, at least in the beginning. Find someone who you know will support you and encourage you.

You also need to believe this vision is your future. When you say "I can't," you are telling yourself a lie. If you never achieve your goals, it won't be due to not having enough money, or from not having enough help from others, or from having bad luck. It will not be due to any real limitation you think you have. It will be because you lied to yourself and said: "I can't." If you get halfway there and no further, it will be because of a limiting self-belief. I cannot stress this enough. The word *believes* is a verb. It is not something that describes you; it is something you do. So do it! When you do, you will be configured for success.

In the succeeding chapters, you will read in more detail about the concept of attraction, about taking action, about surrounding yourself with people, places, and things that will make your dream a reality. When you get in those situations, it is important to already have some idea of your destination; it is important to know what you want. So take the time to discover this vision and to clarify it before moving on. Remember, having no plan means you will wind up nowhere! Knowing what you want is the first step to achieving it.

CHAPTER 17:

THE LAW OF ATTRACTION

As much as we may think we live in a world of the virtual, the electronic, the intellectual – our bodies are real. Our minds are contained within them. In the chapter on waking up and taking action, I will talk about moving your body, getting up and doing something. The mind is the control center for the body. What the body does, everything it does, from feeling pain to the pumping of blood through the heart, even breathing, is controlled by the mind.

If you fill a truck driver with alcohol or cocaine, is the truck going to stay on the road, or even remain intact? Not for very long. The same is true for what we put in our minds and how it affects our bodies. If we fill our minds with thoughts of defeat and failure, it will be very difficult for us to attain victory and success. This concept is not a new one. It is found in the Bible, in Hindu writings, and in the writings of a number of authors since the early nineteenth century.

This philosophy persists because there is truth in it. If you focus on higher things, you will be drawn to them, and they will be drawn to you. The opposite is also true: if you focus on bad things, bad things will come to you. This focus affects the mind in the same way that alcohol affects the driver. And the mind affects the body as the driver affects the truck.

You may be thinking that even if the trucker analogy makes sense, how can what I focus on affect things outside of my body – other people, situations, jobs? The energy in the mind, whether it is positive or negative, attracts similar energy – like attracts like. But in more practical terms, this concept works for everyone, and is constantly at work in the minds and bodies of others. Can you imagine that two people focusing on the same thing might wind up in the same place or situation? While you think about that, I will go over some of the many aspects of life in which the Law of Attraction operates, and explain how your life can change in each of these ways.

Attitude

This is where it all starts. In aviation, attitude (not *altitude*) refers to the orientation of an aircraft, whether it is flying straight and level, or in a bank, or in a dive, or in a climb. It refers, basically, to how it approaches the air, and how it will respond to the air. If you set your attitude to climb, then you will climb over obstacles in your path. You will be pointed toward higher levels of whatever it is you are facing. Attitude is the R (response) in Jack Canfield's E + R = O formula (see Chapter 16: Wake Up and Take Action).

How do you get and keep a good and healthy attitude? The concept of attraction at its most basic level is that "like attracts like." If you want to have a great attitude, put yourself in a community of people with great attitudes. If you focus on this community, it will form around *you*! But do not just sit and wait for this to happen. Look for people with a positive attitude toward life. There are probably some around you now, in your life, at your church, school, or work. Get to know these people and make them your allies in attraction. The power of two or more positive people will draw others even faster.

Remember that attitude is something you need to maintain and care for on a daily basis. Use the concepts you learned in Chapter 13: Have an Attitude for Thinking. Expect to win. These attitudes drive your success throughout each day. The like-minded people you associate with and assemble around you will ensure that you keep this fire burning in your mind.

Behavior

Habits are extremely important. If you change your habits, you change your life. It is more than a cliché to say that we are creatures of habit. Bad habits hurt us. But good habits can be even more powerful in driving us toward the success we desire. Strong habits are difficult to break. Ask anyone who has tried to quit smoking. But good habits can help you stay on the right track even when you are tempted to falter or are not at your best for some reason.

Mornings are a good example of one of these times. Some of us have difficulty getting started in the morning. But if you develop a habit of rising immediately when your alarm goes off, and doing all of the things you need to do, such as reviewing your goal and vision, setting your attitude to superb, brushing your teeth and taking a shower, these things will happen with almost no effort at all.

The Law of Attraction is a law because it always works. This means that if you get into a behavior that is negative, it will obediently send negative things your way. If you tend to whip out your Smartphone and start texting or checking your Facebook messages in the middle of a face-to-face conversation with someone, that negative behavior will come back to you, perhaps in others ignoring you in the same way. If you often lean on your car horn in traffic, that habitual negative habit will attract annoyances for you as well.

In order to start achieving the good things you have envisioned, develop habits of good behavior. Opening doors for people carrying packages. Giving your bus seat to a pregnant woman or elderly person. Write thank-you notes to people who help you. And these good behaviors do not always need to be directed at others. Dress well and appropriately. Exercise several times a week. Take a shower in the morning. Good behavior attracts good behavior and good things.

Friends

As much as I believe that my own success is driven by the spark within me, betting on me does not mean that I do not value or need others. You need friends to support you. And the right kind of friends. I don't mean you should be snobbish or exclusive. But you must choose your friends, and choose wisely because they will impact you. Find a person that has what you want to have, whether that is health, wealth, happiness, or love.

How do you find friends such as this? According to the Law of Attraction, you will attract what you have and what you are. Focus on balance, if you want balance. You will attract friends who value financial success as well as personal health and good works. If two people are focused on the same thing, they will inevitably wind up in the same place. And most importantly, develop a detailed vision (see Chapter 14: Plan for Life Success) that includes your ideal friends. What do they look like? Do they call you every day, or wait until you call?

Maybe you have an old friend who is always complaining. Complaining is attractive in a way and a tempting negative behavior. You may be friends because of the things you have been through together. But if you continue to spend time with this person and this friend will not change, you will attract more people with negative attitudes, and this complaining attitude will infect you as well. Remember that like attracts like. If you are dwelling on the bad things you complain about, you are sure to get more of them!

Friendship should be treated in the same way as diet. You would not put poison in your body because it would kill you. Bad friendships kill your potential happiness. Good friendships support your vision.

One way of expressing this concept is to say that *you are the average of those around you.* Envision a circle of friends who are what you want to be, who do what you want to do, and who have what you want to have. Then welcome them with open arms and share your vision.

Just because you seek out people that have what you want does not mean you are a one-way, selfish person, all take and no give. All good friendships are mutually supportive. My favorite example of how this works is in mentoring and teaching relationships. Why do PhDs teach at universities? Just to make money? I do not think so. Some enjoy it, and that is reason enough. However, I am sure that many would rather just do research and write. Teaching is a two-way street. Both professor and student learn and improve themselves.

You may have already experienced this phenomenon. But if not, give it a test. Take something you know something about, but not a topic on which you are an expert. Now explain that subject to someone else. Afterwards, note how confident you are in the knowledge of what you just taught. Being a mentor is as beneficial as being a student. Do not discount your own strengths as well. Even if someone else has what you want, you may have something that someone wants as well. This is a good basis for a positive, vision-reinforcing friendship.

Do not forget that friendship should also involve fun. And visualizing your dream should be fun as well. It should not be a dreaded task that you perform as an obligation. It should be fun and exciting, something you relish and look forward to. Otherwise, you won't attract happiness, but dread. Make your friendships fun and exciting as well.

Dreams

If you do not know that the place where you are going exists, it will be impossible to get there. When that school counselor told me I would not amount to anything, and I believed it, I was set up not to succeed. It was not until Dr. Sahney showed me what I could be and have that I was able to start moving in a better direction. Now, I create my own dreams. There are no limits to them. When I dream of success, I can see it and it becomes possible to achieve it.

Dream without limits. Go out and find ways to increase your knowledge of what is possible. Then dream even bigger. Bet on yourself. Do not let others limit what is possible for you. The dream, now firmly placed in your mind, becomes an attractive force, and dream will become a reality, if you put in the hard work to get there. If you have trouble reaching beyond the limits of what surrounds you, imagine something better. Whatever you are thinking about, a spouse, friend, car, house, and job – just imagine that there might be something better out there, and dream of that better something, even if you cannot picture it.

Chapter 14 guided you through the creation of your personal vision in several aspects of your life. But dreams can accost you outside the walls of your planning room. Embrace them. You may see an ambulance driving by and dream of becoming a surgeon, or of funding a new wing to a hospital. You may see a beach on a television commercial and dream of owning a house by the sea. You may see a movie about space travel and dream of becoming an astronaut.

Embrace these dreams, and remember that if you can conceive it, and believe it, you can achieve it! Keep the vision in mind and feel the emotions you would feel if it actually happened. A study was done in which world-class runners were asked to run their events in their minds while being monitored for brain activity. The study showed that the brain of each athlete behaved exactly the same way as when the athlete was actually running the race. If you feel as if you have what you already want, your mind will see that state as the state you need to maintain, and begin to attract what is necessary for you to do just that.

Once you understand the Law of Attraction, you may be concerned about thinking the wrong thing and attracting something that you really do not want. A couple of principles should put you at ease. One is that positive thoughts are more powerful than negative ones. The other is that emotions are a more powerful and direct way to access the positive thoughts that will attract your vision.

When you dream, feel all of the emotions of the reality of that dream. Your joy, your excitement, your exhilaration. If your dream includes a sports car, feel the thrill of having your hands on the wheel, your body in the bucket seat, your foot on the pedal as you wind through a curvy road. Hear the sound of the engine and feel your heart pound in response. Feel the adrenaline pumping and your focus narrowing as your speed increases. Make it real and it will become real.

Wealth

Rarely will you find someone with great wealth who never believed they could be wealthy. It just does not happen. Who do you want to be? Where do you want to live? How do you want to spend your time? Financial wealth can make these dreams possible, but only if you can envision yourself in those dreams. Don't just think about that luxurious car you see on a television advertisement. Imagine yourself driving it, or even better, being driven in it, enjoying a clear view of the sky through the panoramic roof or open top. Now, look around you. Suddenly you will find that those cars are closer to you. All around you, in fact.

Have you ever noticed that the rich get richer? This is because like attracts like. There is an infinite abundance of wealth available only to those who envision themselves wealthy. Remember, you *are* wealthy because you *already* have everything you need to get what you want. Keep your wealth in mind. Rise every morning and look at that picture of yourself in a tailored suit or custom-designed evening gown. Imagine it is dawn and the steward has gently awakened you on your yacht. He takes you above decks to have a light breakfast as you enjoy watching a magnificent sunrise with your companion. Imagine moving markets with your stock trades. It is yours. All you have to do is conceive it and believe it.

Success

Whatever you aim for in life, you can achieve. But first you have to believe, you have to focus on the concept in your mind. The mind, properly focused, will drive you toward your goal. It will drive others toward you to help you arrive at your destination and cheer you along the way. It will bring into your hands the tools you need to accomplish your goal. If you want to be an airline captain, imagine yourself piloting a big jet at sixty thousand feet. Then imagine getting there through hard work and study, but never lose sight of the end goal. If you want to be the founder of a charity that changes the world by helping others, imagine that. Visualize yourself doing the job. Put that image firmly in your mind. Focus it, look at all the details. Make it real.

When I was working in the corporate world, I put limits on my success. It was always the job I was currently doing. Because I did not conceive of anything more, I did not achieve anything more. Still, I was very successful. I was fortunate. Even then, the Law of Attraction was working in my life, because all I could see was a project, the project's kept coming to me. I was focused on this level. Imagine if I had raised my gaze upward, had focused on what I *could* be, and not just what I was at that moment?

Just as the rich get richer, the successful get more successful. The more success you have, the more it is a part of your experience, the easier it is to envision, and most importantly, to *feel* that success and all the emotions tied up with it.

Success only comes to those who envision it. It is necessary to wake up and take action, to work hard. But even this is not enough unless you can see the destination in your mind. See it, and the attractive force will drive you toward success, will drive your dream right back at you. The next chapter is about the hard work you will need to do to achieve your goals. You will know what you need to do—the Law of Attraction will bring those tasks to you and set them right in front of you. Act on them immediately. The universe has no speed limit. You are only limited by the acts you choose not to take and how you carry them out.

Lynn F. Austin

CHAPTER 18:

OUTCOMES

> He put a new song in my mouth, a hymn of praise to
> our God. Many will see and fear the LORD and put
> their trust in him. Psalm 40:3

Working hard was part of my auto-piloted success by accident. But working hard is not bad. It is necessary for success. Hard work alone will get you somewhere, but not necessarily where you want to be. Paired with a plan for a successful life, hard work will be the driving force for your success.

There is an old riddle that is appropriate here. Three frogs sit on a log. One of them decides to jump off the log into the water and start swimming. How many frogs are left sitting on the log? The answer is: three. Just making a decision did not propel the frog forward. He still needs to take action to do what he has already decided to do. When your plan is complete, and your attitude is configured for success, you still need to put your body in motion.

In my case, I had a lot of action without a complete plan. The result was not what is should have been or could have been. You may have a lot of plans that you never seem to get accomplished. The result of this kind of philosophy with no action is also not what you desire. Jack Canfield uses a formula to describe this:

Event + Response = Outcome

Or

E + R = O

You can find his description of this on JackCanfield.com. It is easy to blame the event (E) for your result (O). E is what happens to you, not what you have done or not done. For example, my parents did not support me enough (E), therefore I am unable to succeed in life (O). But here I have completely left out the R, which is my response to how my parents did or did not support me. The key here is that in every situation, no matter how far beyond you it seems, R is a necessary component of the equation. There is no Outcome without your Response, even if you choose not to respond and your Response is zero. It follows that you have a measure of control over every Outcome. E can be beyond your control, but R is one hundred percent in your control.

The Outcome is always dependent on how you respond, how much effort you invest, how well you prepare, how quickly you react – all things you control. If you choose not to act and blame the Event, you can't expect the Outcome you want.

In the above situation, choosing not to act, you were awake and aware that your Response was a necessary component of your Outcome. That's called waking up. And once you have awoken, it's difficult to find excuses for not having a successful Outcome.

Remember that you are betting on yourself now. You cannot have the success I am talking about, the wealth, relationships, or anything else you envision unless you take one hundred percent of the responsibility for your life. If you have been a complainer, you must retire from the blame game. Make your Response the one that brings you the Outcome that matches your personal vision.

As I alluded to in the chapter on the Law of Attraction, you will know what to do, because you will get inspirations. They will seem like random thoughts that come into your mind, but they are messages. When you envision your dream, your ideal life, your brain goes to work making that dream come true, especially if you practice feeling the emotions you will feel when it does come true. The brain is sending messages, and messages come back. When they do, act on them as soon as possible.

At first, this will seem unusual. It won't feel comfortable. It might even feel dangerous. But it is important to get over this fear and act on these messages. You may be driving and see two small road signs with arrows pointing at a turn, like a double arrow, and be inspired to take that turn. Just take it. You'll never know what is down that road unless you go there. Or you may be in a grocery store, and something tells you to speak to a particular person. Tell them "hello" or ask about the weather, or talk about whatever you are inspired to talk about. You may have an image of a friend pop into your head and just stay there as you go about your day. Call that friend and tell them you love them (if you do), or whatever else you feel inspired to say.

You will be amazed when your actions lead to big jumps in your progress. If the message has to go through all of the gatekeepers you have set up in your brain, the opportunity may be lost or delayed. Make that phone call, check the PO Box, and take that turn down a new road--whatever the message tells you to do.

CHAPTER 19:

ACCOUNTABILITY

If you take *The BOM* seriously, then you have only one boss. YOU. The boss takes responsibility. As Harry Truman said, "The buck stops here." That means, whatever happens, you take responsibility and don't blame anyone else. But being the boss also means you are *accountable*. If life doesn't go according to your plan, it is your plan, so you must accept this, and adjust accordingly. If your plan succeeds, congratulate yourself. You are accountable for wins as well as losses!

It is important to be accountable on a daily basis because success depends on good habits, and habits can improve or deteriorate over time. They also need vigilance in their establishment. For example, having a good attitude. Everyone has bad days and good days, but if you don't start with an attitude aimed at success, you have zero chance of achieving it. If you do start with that attitude, you cannot avoid achieving it, through obstacles may present themselves more forcefully during a "bad" day.

If you are a parent or know parents, you understand the concern for your children's associations. You want to know who they spend their time with. Why? Because they are affected by those other children, who are affected in turn by whoever they are spending time with. The same is true for anyone, adults included. Be accountable for the choices you make about who is around you. You become the average of those you associate with. If you associate with billionaires, and you are not one, you will be on your way to great financial wealth. If you associate with people in happy, fulfilling relationships, your relationships will become more happy and fulfilling.

The concept that you are the average of the people around you seems obvious when you think about it. But accountability means you need to evaluate at times the groups you are a part of, the people you are with. It is so easy to sit at the complainer's table on a lunch break at work. Sometimes it seems like there is nothing more satisfying than griping and whining about whatever is going on at work. There is always something to complain about. But if you are reading this book, you are not a complainer; you are not a whiner. You don't blame the event when the outcome does not suit you. You have retired from the blame game. You are accountable, and you go right to work on your response to the event, and you make the outcome you want.

You don't belong in the complainer's group. Sit at the table with those who talk about their dreams and inspirations, and about facing obstacles and finding ways to vault over them or get around them. Be accountable.

Another reason that accountability is important on a daily basis is that nothing good comes instantly. Ask anyone who has been lauded as an "overnight success," and they will tell you it took lots of overnights, and lots of hard work to achieve that success. Sam Goldwyn said, "Give me a couple of years, and I'll make that actress an overnight success." Success and work are married, for better or better. And that work is done in smaller steps. The little things, day after day. They seem tedious, but they are all looking toward a final accomplishment that is exactly what you envision it to be. If you want plump, delicious tomatoes in June, you have to plant them in March and water them, mulch them and weed them on a regular basis. What you do on a daily basis determines the outcome. Accountability means you do the little things and hold yourself responsible for doing them. Remember, you are the boss!

Buddha says a jug is filled drop by drop. Continued accountability is extremely important. I wrote this book one word at a time. Even one letter at a time. I would never be a published author if I had tried to write my books all at once. There is no such thing as overnight success, but there is such a thing as success. There is no such thing as getting rich quick (thought it might happen quicker than you previously thought possible), but there is such a thing as getting rich.

At this point, your task may seem daunting. You may be discouraged and think that you cannot be successful, it is too much work. I am here to tell you that you can be successful. I continue to find success and you can too. I have some tools that will help you be accountable so you can accomplish the little things.

Focus.

Like the driver who keeps his or her central vision on the horizon, keeps your thoughts focused on your personal vision at all times. It should become a part of you, so that every task is seen as a step toward that goal.

When I say focus, I don't mean that you should be a day-dreamer, always with your head in the sky. You need to have a clear focus on your immediate task. But when you understand that doing this work will get you to your ultimate goal, it will inspire you to work even harder to finish your current task.

Build Habits. Habits are strong because they use the sub-conscious mind. Have you ever noticed that while your mind has wandered, you have completed part or all of some habitual task? This often happens to people who are driving the same route they drive every day. They will suddenly realize that they have driven for miles and do not remember doing it. That is how strong habits are. Use this concept to your advantage. Make habits of the tasks that keep you accountable, like measuring your progress, and focusing on long-term and intermediate goals.

Break it Down. Large tasks can be daunting until you recognize that they are done one step at a time. Once you are aware of your next task, ask yourself what smaller tasks need to be done to accomplish it. Schedule them and check them off when complete.

Get an Accountability Buddy. You might also call this person your "partner in crime." The best case is someone who is on a similar path, who has a vision herself and is working to achieve it. But anyone who will be supportive and hold your feet to the fire will do. All that is required is that they ask you about your progress. And it should be someone you cannot fool also.

This is a small list of the tools you can use to help yourself be accountable. Remember that every race you win begins with a first step and is won one step at a time. But you need to stay on the track for the whole race. This is what accountability is all about.

Lynn F. Austin

CHAPTER 20:

PERSISTENCE AND PERSEVERANCE

When I gave the commencement speech at my college graduation, I spoke about how doing the little things on a daily basis is what brings the big things to fruition. It is easy for students graduating to understand this. Only days or weeks before graduation, they are working on final assignments to turn in which must be completed prior to graduation. Little things. Then the big thing comes fast. It is scheduled. They know it is coming. Most of the time, it takes a little more effort than this to stay focused on your goals. But there are several concepts I have found that will help you to keep your eye on the big things.

The most important thing to keep in mind as you progress through life's challenges and rewards is that spark inside you. Whatever you do or become, it has more to do with what is inside you than anyone else or any event or situation outside of you. Perhaps you never had an experience like the one I had in New Orleans, but you do not need one. No magic is required for you to realize the truly amazing person you are. I am not an alien being or something supernatural. I am a human being. So are you. So I know that if I have that spark, that light inside, then you have it too. You may not think of it in the same way. In fact, you probably don't. We are each unique. But it is important to remember that you have the ability to drive yourself to success, and no one can take that away from you. Including you! Say to yourself "I'm going to bet on me. Because I am the best bet for success."

If you have read Chapters 13 and 14, then you have an attitude and a plan for success. In order to keep these going, I find it helpful to focus on them specifically and intentionally on a daily basis. Write them or print them on a piece of paper and put them somewhere so that you cannot miss looking at them in the morning. That way you start your day already focused on your goals, and in the right frame of mind to progress toward accomplishing them.

In order to be persistent enough to achieve your vision, whatever it is, you need to be able to deal with adversity. So many fail because they are unwilling to go on risking repeated failure after a setback. You need to find the inspiration to do that. Something personal that drives you to keep trudging through the bad times. Otherwise, you may not have the strength to go forward, and if you don't continue moving, you will never reach your vision.

My favorite story about persistence is the story of Abraham Lincoln. It can be found in the book *Chicken Soup for the Soul* by Jack Canfield and Mark Victor Hansen. You can also find it on www.ChickenSoup.com. Here are the essential events from the life of the sixteenth president:

1816	His family was forced out of their home. He had to work to support them. He was seven years old.
1818	His mother died.
1831	Failed in business.
1832	Ran for state legislature — lost.
1832	Also lost his job — wanted to go to law school but couldn't get in.
1833	Borrowed some money from a friend to begin a business and by the end of the year, he was bankrupt. He spent the next 17 years of his life paying off this debt.
1834	Ran for state legislature again — won.
1835	Was engaged to be married, sweetheart died, and his heart was broken.
1836	Had a total nervous breakdown and was in bed for six months.
1838	Sought to become speaker of the state legislature — defeated.
1840	Sought to become elector — defeated.
1843	Ran for Congress — lost.

1846	Ran for Congress again — this time he won — went to Washington and did a good job.
1848	Ran for re-election to Congress — lost.
1849	Sought the job of land officer in his home state — rejected.
1854	Ran for Senate of the United States — lost.
1856	Sought the Vice Presidential nomination at his party's national convention — got less than 100 votes.
1858	Ran for U.S. Senate again — again he lost.
1860	Elected president of the United States.

This was a man who is widely considered to be the greatest or one of the greatest presidents in American history. Imagine what the United States would be like if he had quit after losing the election in 1958? Or at any of the many times in his life that he faced failure and negative circumstances?

Ray Allen holds the record for most career three-point field goals made in the NBA, almost 3,000. He is also the most accurate three-point shooter of all-time: he hits forty percent of his attempts. But this means he also misses sixty percent of his shots. In fact, he has missed more three-point shots than any other NBA player, almost 4500! He misses fifty percent more three-pointers than he makes. Yet he has built an amazing career full of records, most notably in this area of performance. What if Ray Allen got dejected after every miss and did not try again? He would not have achieved the success he has achieved. He has to keep shooting and keep missing in order to succeed. So must you!

Enjoy life! Don't be convinced that just because you have not achieved your ultimate goal yet, you cannot be happy. Insist on happiness on a daily basis, right here, right now. Though it may seem strange, maintaining your happiness is a big part of your success. It is important to persevere in happiness. Continue to feel the emotions of one who is already in possession of his vision – because you already possess everything you need to achieve it. Know that your vision is going to become reality. All it takes is hard work, perseverance and the ability to never lose sight of that vision. Keep it in sight through failures and setbacks. The road to success is not an easy one. So the presence of those jagged rocks is sure proof that you are headed in the right direction.

This is the final lesson I have for you, because it is extremely important, and I want you to remember it as you trudge the daily path toward the great things that I know will happen if you persist and persevere.

My own vision has driven me to write this book. It is a vision of many people achieving their dreams. They have achieved them by accepting that everything that happens to them happens for them, and betting on themselves. They have found the spark inside them, and it has enlightened their vision. Through hard work and unrelenting focus, they have trudged through challenges to reach their ultimate visions. My hope is that you are one of them. I invite you to visit my website and share your story as I have shared mine with you. And I wish for you only the best as you continue your journey. And always remember to Bet On Me for success!

Made in the USA
San Bernardino, CA
23 November 2018